SOCCER: THE FUNDAMENTALS

BARBARA BONNEY

The Rourke Press, Inc.
Vero Beach, Florida 32964

PHOTO CREDITS
© Karen Weisman: pages 9, 16; © American Youth Soccer Organization: pages 4, 6, 12; © Glen Benson : cover, pages 7, 10, 13, 15, 18, 19, 21, 22

ACKNOWLEDGMENTS
The author wishes to acknowledge Doug Semark for his contribution in writing this book.

EDITORIAL SERVICES:
Penworthy Learning Systems

Library of Congress Cataloging-in-Publication Data

Bonney, Barbara, 1955-
   Soccer: The fundamentals / Barbara Bonney.
     p. cm. — (Soccer)
   Includes index.
   Summary: An overview of the game of soccer including its history, the spirit of the game, coaching, conditioning, and mental preparation required for playing.
   ISBN 1-57103-138-3
   1. Soccer—Juvenile literature. [1. Soccer.]
I. Title II. Series: Bonney, Barbara, 1955- Soccer.
GV943.25.B65 1997
796.334—DC21   97-8099
                                      CIP
                                      AC

Printed in the USA

TABLE OF CONTENTS

The History of Soccer 5

The Spirit of the Game 6

Coaches 8

Teams 11

Games 12

Referees 14

Conditioning 17

Mental Preparation 18

Playing the Ball 20

Glossary 23

Index 24

THE HISTORY OF SOCCER

Since ancient times, ball-kicking games have been played all over the world. Many of these games were violent. By the 1860's, the English tamed the sport for use in schools. For the first time rules were made for everyone to follow. People disagreed over the rules for carrying the ball and kicking players on purpose. People decided to keep those rules in a game called **rugby** (RUG bee) but not in soccer. In soccer, which is called football in most countries, the ball cannot be touched by hands and people cannot be violent.

Italians have played a violent ball-kicking game called "calico" for centuries.

Soccer is played all over the world.

THE SPIRIT OF THE GAME

Soccer is different from every other sport. In most sports the goal is to win while following many rules. In soccer, **sportsmanship** (SPORTS mun ship) is important for players, coaches, and referees. The rules, or laws, of soccer are not as important as playing a game

People of all sizes play soccer.

Having fun is just part of playing soccer.

that is safe, fair, and fun. Players must show respect for the laws and the referee. Also, the referee must respect the spirit of the game.

COACHES

The coach is the leader of a soccer team. A coach's job is to help the players learn skills through practice. A coach helps the players work together as a team, too. Sometimes this job means trying new plays or moving players to different positions. A good coach pushes all team members to do their best, not just a few good players. Players who show up on time for practice and listen to instructions help their coaches.

Coaches give instructions before a game.

TEAMS

Kids' soccer teams join to form **leagues**
(LEEGZ) that may belong to state or national
organizations. Being part of a larger group is
helpful for getting uniforms and equipment,
training coaches, and having **tournaments**
(TUR neh mentz). Being on a team means more
than these things, though. A team is not just a
collection of kids who play soccer. If each player
plays like he or she is alone, the team will not
work. If players try to help and learn from each
other, they are more likely to succeed. Success
takes practice and cooperation.

Linespersons are now called
assistant referees.

Teams that work well together might play in tournaments.

GAMES

A soccer season usually runs in the spring and fall. In colder climates games may be played on indoor soccer fields. The indoor rules are a little different from outdoor soccer. In warmer climates, soccer can be played year-round.

Each half of outdoor soccer games is 25 minutes or less.

Good sportsmanship is more important than who wins.

Outdoor soccer games have 25-minute halves, less time for younger players. Half-time is at least five minutes. The referee stops the timer only for half-time.

REFEREES

Each soccer game has a referee who controls it. A referee's job is to keep time and score, stop play for injuries, and allow **substitutions** (SUB steh TOO shunz). A referee also stops the game if there is a reason to and makes sure the laws (rules) are followed. Two assistant referees decide when the ball has crossed the touchlines. The referee blows the whistle for fouls. A referee is also in the game to teach players the rules of soccer and how to play the game.

A coach is often a father or mother.

The referee calls for substitutes.

CONDITIONING

Conditioning (kun DISH uh ning) is important before playing any sport. Running is a good way to get your body ready for soccer. Start with a short distance; then add a minute or two each day. Other good exercises are moving a soccer ball with your feet and running with the ball near your feet. Between games, team practice is a good way to condition. Before each practice and game most teams do warm-ups, or stretching exercises, to prepare their bodies for running and kicking. Warm-ups prevent injuries.

Stretching legs before a game helps prevent injuries.

MENTAL PREPARATION

Just as bodies need conditioning and warm-ups, the mind needs to be prepared for a game. Soccer is not just a physical sport. Good players are alert during practice and games. They exercise their minds by always thinking about

Listening to the referee helps everybody learn.

Good coaches give their team a positive attitude.

where the ball is and how they can help their team to score. Good players also try to understand the game by listening to the coach and referee.

PLAYING THE BALL

In soccer the ball may be controlled and played several ways—always without touching it with hands or arms. Often feet are used. When a player runs while controlling the ball with his or her feet, it's called **dribbling** (DRIB ling). A kick can be used to move the ball a long distance or into the goal. A kick to a teammate is called a pass. Stopping the ball is called trapping, which is done with feet, shins, knees, and chest. When a ball is bounced off of a player's head it is called heading.

Practice makes players and teams better.

Dribbling is often used to move the ball down the field.

GLOSSARY

conditioning (kun DISH uh ning) — preparing the body and mind with exercises for work or play, such as a soccer game

dribbling (DRIB ling) — to move a ball by repeated light kicks

leagues (LEEGZ) — a group of teams that compete with each other

rugby (RUG bee) — a game similar to football and soccer named after a school in England

sportsmanship (SPORTS mun ship) — fair play and a good attitude

substitutions (SUB steh TOO shunz) — players who are put in a game in place of other players

tournaments (TUR neh mentz) — a series of contests that one team wins

Soccer involves a lot of running.

INDEX

coach   6, 8, 11, 19

conditioning   17, 18

dribbling   20

half-time   13

heading   20

indoor soccer   12

laws   6, 7, 14

leagues   11

outdoor soccer   12, 13

pass   20

referee   6, 7, 13, 14, 19

rugby   5

season   12

sportsmanship   6, *13*

substitutions   14

tournaments   11

trapping   20

warm-ups   17